Pumpkin Art

PHOTOGRAPHS BY
Maddie Levine

Verse By Philip Macht

Ann & Sandy, Thank you for all your support Maddie

Maxrom Press/Baltimore

Maddie Levine:
Stephanie and Bobby
my inspiration and my anchor

* * * * * * * * * * * * *

Philip Macht:

For Madeleine, Sarah,
Eloise, and Danny

* * * * * * * * * * * * *

Library of Congress Card Catalog Number: 91-61689
ISBN: 0-930339-02-9

Published in the United States by:
Maxrom Press, 11 East Fayette Street
Baltimore, Maryland 21202

Printed in the U.S.A.   First Edition

Consider the pumpkin:
In natural state the curves are expansive —
The color is great.

Snuggled down tight,
      no two are alike.

Go out in the field on an October day.
Wander among them, enjoy the display.

But after the harvest
   you may have some problems.
Problems with pumpkins and
   how do you solve them.
No matter how much you
   do truly love them —
When the weather's been good,
   there are too many of them.

First, sell what you can to the Roadside Gourmet.
Then call up your friends — try to give some away.

Then mince 'em or stew 'em,
   do anything to 'em.
Boil and reduce 'em,
   soup 'em and juice 'em.
Spice 'em and grill 'em,
   try to distill 'em.
Slice 'em and fry 'em,
   and certainly pie 'em.

You can have pumpkin most any way.
But after you've had it 'most every day
And feel that you're starting to hate them —
Decorate them . . .
Recreate them . . .
Animate them.

Try out your painting —
   they're perfect for faces.
Try out your knife —
   and light up the spaces.

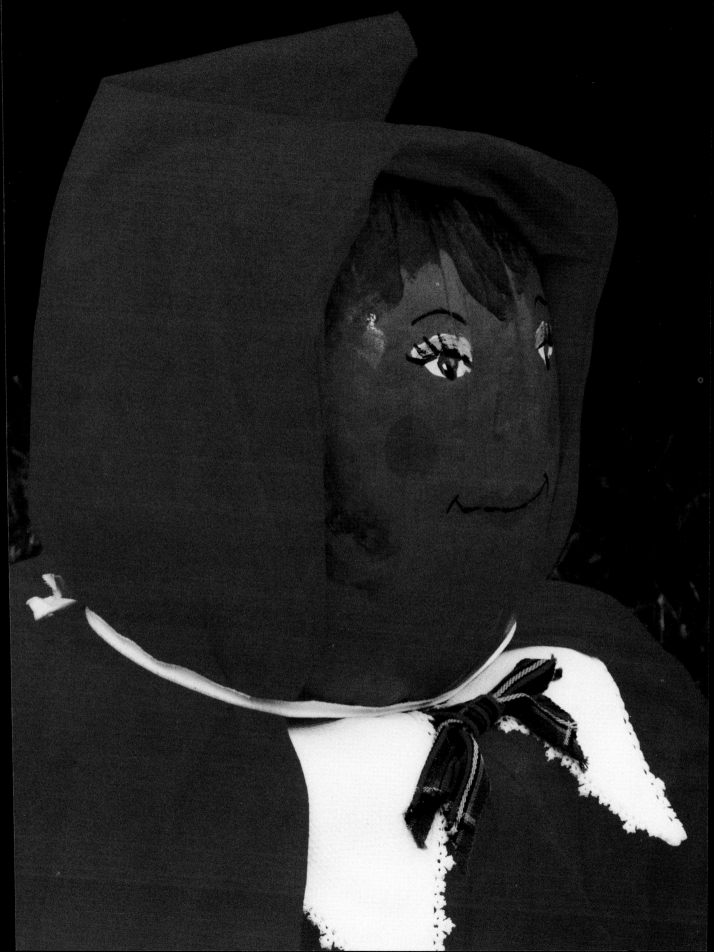

Comic or tragic —
   invest them with magic.